Eerie Planet

Marquis H.K.

Eerie Planet, Marquis H.K.

Published by

Dark Moon Press

P.O. Box 11496

Fort Wayne, Indiana 46858-1496

ISBN-13: 978-0

BISAC: Photography

www.DarkMoonPress.com

Table of Contets

Acknowledgements

The following people are owed my eternal gratitude for their part in making this project come to fruition. Paul 'Stoney' Stone and OTP Graphics for amazing cover artwork. My brother Jim Azazel Blake for help with layout and being a true left-hand path comrade. Robin Fassbender. Chris 'Skumbo' Furphy, Gavin Baddeley, Simon Gilberthorpe.

For the road trips – Petr Dostal and Eva (Castle Houska), Helen Harley (Clophill), Laurence Sellick (Boleskine House), my Uncle Bernard (Saddleworth Moor). All the people I've met whilst visiting these amazing places. And anyone who has supported this project in any way, shape, or form.

Ave

Introduction

Writing and compiling material for this book was certainly no easy undertaking. It involved around seven years of travel between the years of 2011 – 2017. And whilst travelling is a very exciting, adventurous experience, it can also be a very costly venture. Especially from Australia, where I began this project. This is why most of the research was conducted whilst spending time in the UK between 2016 – 2017. The reason being that most of the locations within these pages are either located in the UK or in Europe where distance is more easily accessible and affordable financially.

It was never originally my intention to write a book on the places I've visited. Just like most people I had a 'list' of places I wanted to see and the more I learnt about other places the more I kept adding to it. However, as things were gradually crossed off the list over the years someone put the idea to me to write a book about all the dark places in history I've visited and my impressions of them so here we are.

The list is by no means complete and there are many other places on this planet with a dark history which I'd love to visit and document. I may well do this in a second edition of this project. Only time will tell I've always had a fascination with the esoteric, paranormal and blood thirsty figures in history. So here are just a few places that have a definite connection to the aforementioned subjects that have left a lasting impression on me. Enjoy.

Marquis H.K.

The Hell-Fire Caves

ighteenth century England there existed a secret society devote
idden pleasure and carnal delights. They were an aristocratic bu
prising of powerful members of society, mainly politicians.

y would meet in a secret location and engage in hedonistic indulg
blasphemous activity. This allegedly included black masses, c
ship, excessive drinking and lustful orgies. They were basic

British high born gentlemen seeking a life of forbidden excitement by flirting with danger and the unknown. Challenging the moral code of Christianity and questioning the ethics of the church by adopting the role of sinful monks. They were on a mission to fulfil the ultimate form of gratification by indulging in the highest form of hedonistic pleasure.

This esoterical group of individuals came to be known as the Hellfire Club. The ring-leader or key player was Sir Francis Dashwood who was Chancellor of the Exchequer at the time and acted as high priest at these meetings toasting the devil and other hellish deities. Other members included poet and political satirist Paul Whitehead, the Earl of Sandwich, and Member of Parliament John Wilkes. Benjamin Franklin was also a good friend of Dashwoods and visited the caves on several occasions. The meetings would involve role play dress ups taken from various foreign cultures which inspired Dashwood on his many travels. There was also sexual interaction with various women, some of whom reportedly wore masks to protect their identity. Their initial meeting place was an abandoned medieval abbey in Mendenham where they were known as the 'Friars of Mendenham'.

Dashwood then had caves especially excavated in the chalk hill facing his estate in West Wycombe thus further immersing themselves in secrecy. Dashwood saw this as a double positive because he could combat unemployment by employing local workers to do the digging. The club had dissolved by 1766 and the caves went into a state of disrepair after the heady days were over and its members long gone. No maintenance work has been carried out on them since the eighteenth century. They were still open to public exploration as just another abandoned site but it was only really the locals who knew of their existence. They were in fact going to be used as proposed make shift air

– raid shelters in World War 2 but seeing as Wycombe was never bombed this never occurred.

In 1951 Sir Francis Dashwood (11th Baronet) - a direct descendent of the original Sir Francis, set to work on restoring the caves. This proved to be no small undertaking however and wasn't without its fair share of dangerous accidents, though luckily no fatalities. The restoration of the caves was fully completed and reopened in 1974 and has since proved to be a lucrative business attracting thousands of visitors a year. The caves are located on Church Lane, West Wycombe, High Wycombe, Buckinghamshire. The first thing you notice whilst driving along West Wycombe Hill Road is the hexagonal shaped Mausoleum of Sir Francis Dashwood perched on top of the hill on which the caves are located. It is quite a striking monument and was used for the final scene of the last Hammer House of Horror production 'To the Devil a Daughter'. Starring Christopher Lee it was the movie adaption of the Dennis Wheatley novel.

The centre of the mausoleum used to have a marble urn containing the heart of Paul Whitehead - the Hellfire Club Steward. It was his wish to Sir Francis as a 'parting gift' after his death in 1774. However the heart was stolen by an Australian soldier in 1839 and Whitehead's ghost is said to stalk the grounds of West Wycombe looking for his heart! The marble urn now resides in the safe confines of Paul Whitehead's cavern within the caves. The caves themselves are designed from flint and chalk and the front entrance is designed to look like a gothic church with its medieval arches. You enter through a turnstile and are welcomed with a voice recording of the latest Sir Francis Dashwood explaining the history of the caves. There are also various plaques on the wall with information on club members.

The first port of call at the end of the straight tunnel entrance is the tool store cave. This is stacked with tools similar to the ones used in the original excavation of the eighteenth century – pick axes, hammers, shovels, candles and candle holders. From there begins the descent into darkness through the winding passages to the caverns below. Now it has to be said that this could prove a hindrance for any tall people as some of the arches are really quite low. I'm 5ft 10in and I had to duck down to get through some of them.

It is then we come to the caverns of Lord Sandwich and Paul Whitehead facing opposite each other. Each contains a statue, Sandwich in oriental costume with a baboon that was used as a practical joke on him by fellow club member John Wilkes. Whitehead is sitting at a table writing up the cellar book of wine, as was his job. The original aforementioned urn that contained his heart in the mausoleum sits beside him. The descent gets steeper and darker and you really do get the feeling you're descending into the dark depths of hell. Halfway down there are some Roman numerals inscribed in the wall – XXII. Legend has it that this marks a secret passage leading up to St Lawrence Church on top of the hill next to the mausoleum.

Next is a bit of a maze containing a cave featuring Sir Francis Dashwood and Benjamin Franklin and a Children's Cave featuring Sir George Dashwood and his sister Mary Berkley as children. Next is the Main Banquetting Hall. You are now halfway on your descent. Its 40 feet in diameter with a compass design and contains modern statues from Italy. This is available to hire out for private parties and functions and is definitely on the list for yours truly. Of course the caves have been used in numerous TV productions. Most notably being the subject of UK paranormal investigative production 'Most Haunted', in which the show's team investigates the alleged hauntings of the caves.

Down from the Banquetting Hall is a triangular shape of passageways which lead back to the main path. This allegedly represents the female anatomy. Next is the Miner's Cave where miners are depicted with tools and scaffolding. One then crosses the River Styx which is the border between earth and the underworld. The souls of the dead were said to be ferried across by the Boatman Charon. Then you are here, you've arrived at your infernal destination, the Inner Temple. You are now 300 feet underground beneath St Lawrence Church. Clearly signifying heaven and hell, this is where all the club's meetings and gatherings took place. A place of many forbidden pleasures and revelry! In the temple are statues of Sir Francis, John Wilkes, Lord Sandwich and Charles Churchill against a statue of Venus de Milo entertaining two masked 'lady friends'. If only these walls could talk!

There is only one way in and out of the caves so you have to go back the way you came. However, there is no time limit and you are free to explore the caves as long as you wish. Providing you're out by closing time. At the entrance is a charming little cafe that sells good food and a whole range of books and souvenirs. A great affordable day out and a fine opportunity to explore this dark part of English history.

Main entrance to the caves.

Sir Francis Dashwood Mausoleum.

The author investigates the caves.

The interior of the Sir Francis Dashwood Mausoleum. It once held a marble urn containing the heart of Paul Whitehead and was also the location for the final scene of the movie adaption of the Dennis Wheatley novel *To The Devil A Daughter*.

SIR FRANCIS DASHWOOD
2nd BARONET

Creator of the Hell-Fire Caves and
the notorious Hell-Fire Club

In 1726 Sir Francis embarked on a Grand Tour of Europe
Italy especially aroused a passionate interest in the art and
culture of classical antiquity.
He also acquired there a taste for high living.
For many of his parties he enjoyed dressing up in oriental
costume or even as a monk!
In 1748 he commenced the excavations of the Caves.

Plaque of Sir Francis Dashwood.

List of Hell–Fire Club members.

Wax figures in the Inner Temple in the depths of the caves, where the Hell-Fire Club held their decadent celebrations. Legend has it influential women wore masks to conceal their identity.

The Ruins of St Mary's Church Clophill

Located in Bedfordshire in the south midlands of England lies the sleepy, picturesque village of Clophill. Tucked away at the top of a lonely winding dirt track are the ruins of the old St Mary's Church. It was built around 1350 but was abandoned in 1848 and replaced by a Victorian church in the centre of the village.

Local folklore suggests some very sinister reasons as to why it was abandoned. Some say the church was built the wrong way round facing Satan rather than God. Others say it was built on the site of a former leper hospital run by monks. There certainly has been some sinister activity taken place at the ruins in years gone by. It has been the site of Satanic rituals, Black Masses, grave desecration and paranormal activity. Some have reported seeing ghostly figures and feeling a chilly oppressive atmosphere upon entering the ruins. They were also the subject of a 2010 feature film The *Paranormal Diaries – Clophill* directed by Kevin Gates. The film is part documentary part fiction and is based on actual events. It focuses on a team of researchers who spend three nights at the ruins unintentionally unleashing malevolent forces. Gates has also written a book of the same name documenting its entire history.

To quote: "There was an incident at Clophill one night in March 1963 when the grave of a young woman named Jenny Humberstone was opened up by members of a black magic coven. Her skull and bones were taken into the nave of the church and arranged in a circle on a makeshift altar. Symbols were then scrawled onto the walls and a ceremony conducted which culminated in the sacrifice of a cockerel. A lot of people thought it was a Black Mass but it was actually a ceremony closer to Necromancy. It was at a revivalist time of the occult in the U.K. And the Clophill story featured heavily in the press. For a time the rector of the village, Lewis Barker, was the focus as it had taken place in his parish and for many years believed he had been cursed by the witches of Clophill. The reason being he had kept the bones of Jenny Humberstone in the boot of his car and the witches wanted them back! All very true. "

English punk band U.K. Decay had a paranormal experience in 1979 when they shot the cover for their debut E.P. *The Black 45* at the ruins. The band hail from the nearby town of Luton and thought it an appropriate place to do the photo shoot for the cover. The band suddenly felt spooked and the urge to get the hell out of there. They sped off down the track and encountered a white horse out of nowhere in front of them. They slowed down to let the horse get around the corner. The band weren't five seconds behind when the horse completely vanished! There's nowhere it could have gone or come from, the hedges at the side of the track are too high and dense. They stopped at the village pub The Flying Horse for a pint where they asked the staff if they knew of anyone who owned a white horse that may have escaped. The staff couldn't believe what they had just heard and proceeded to tell them of the local folklore of the phantom white horse!

Guitarist, Spon, shares his Clophill experience: "We had just finished recording our second UK Decay single in October 1979 which we later named 'The Black 45' EP because we had written some of the songs with a horror type theme. We needed a cover for the new single and there was this ruined church on a hill in a nearby village, so we and a photographer set out in a car to get some photos. It was the end of the month around Halloween and a moonlit but cold night as we turned off the main road and drove up the winding track. We parked the car near the entrance porch, got out and prepared ourselves for the photos and shone a torch towards the church. The graveyard with decaying tombs and crumbling gravestones was completely overgrown and a spooky mist seemed to lurk in the shadows of the sunken path leading to the church's entrance. Back in them days it was really like a scene from the Hammer House of Horrors.

We had a job to do so we walked up the path and through the entrance, the door had long disappeared and we walked inside. As the torchlight swept the crumbling walls we could see the graffiti, including pentagrams and the cliched numbers '666' and other stuff scrawled about the place. All the windows had gone, so all four of us got up onto the bottom of one of the former windows and we posed whilst our photographer climbed amongst the gravestones to get a decent angle for the shots.

So we were standing there looking towards our photographer with the flash temporary blinding us. We were there for a few minutes trying different poses and shots. We were all in our late teens or early twenties, so I guess we were highly excitable. As there were five of us we didn't feel particularly afraid, but as time wore on and more shots taken and the fact we were balancing on a wall a metre or two high in the dark with the blinding flashes soon led to a disorientation. Then someone thought they heard movement from within the church behind us. This soon amplified as our eyes blinded by the flash couldn't see anything, our ears were either playing tricks or there was something moving behind us. Before long, almost spontaneously, we all jumped off the wall and fled back to the car in blind panic.

We started the car and quickly headed back down the old hollow lane which was sunken with high hedges each side. We soon picked up speed and rounding the bend the car came to a screeching halt as the headlights lit up a magnificent rider-less white horse strolling down the lane in front of us. Our hearts were pounding and we looked at each other, "Is that for real"? We had all seen it! After a moment the horse disappeared round the bend a few yards further along. With that we pulled off again, I think we assumed it must have been an escaped horse. Within moments we reached the bend and could clearly see right down the lane again. There was absolutely no sign of the horse, neither any obvious place it could have escaped the confines of the track in the short time it took to round the bend! The hedgerows were dense and over ten feet high with no gates! The horse had vanished before our very eyes!

We were really spooked by this and couldn't stop talking about it for days afterwards. None of us could see anywhere a white horse that size could have moved out of view that quickly. Of course it could have been a real escaped white horse. We will never really know but it certainly had an effect on the band's music. There was to our minds a genuine 'oddness' about the incident.

A number of years later I told the story of the white horse to a local who grew up near Clophill in mid-Bedfordshire and he was not surprised. He told me that the 'ghostly' white horse was a well-known local legend of the Clophill Village and the surrounding area. And reminded me that the name of the local village pub was 'The Flying Horse'".

The ruins are now owned by The Clophill Heritage Trust, a volunteer group who purchased the building and had it restored. The occult graffiti has been removed and a spiral staircase and observation platform installed in the tower. I visited the ruins with a friend from London in November 2014. We drove up the creepy Old Church Path and upon arrival were met with a huge fence and 'Keep Out' sign in front of the iconic ruin. My instant reaction was "Bollocks! I've come all the way from Australia to see this"! So we made our way around the perimeter of the undergrowth and got some photos.

We were met with a bemused member of the trust who lives in the eco lodge across the path. He informed us we'd turned up after opening hours. It seems they also want to rid the church of its dark and supernatural past. Stating that morbid curiosity seekers are getting quite 'tiresome'. Well good luck with that! In all seriousness what do you honestly expect? If you're going to purchase anything with a dark or notorious past then you really should be capitalising on it. I think he realised this when another car load pulled up for exactly the same reason!

Old Church Path leading up to the ruins.

An orb?

Clophill in its former state covered in Satanic graffiti.

UK Decays "Black 45" EP with cover shot at Clophill.

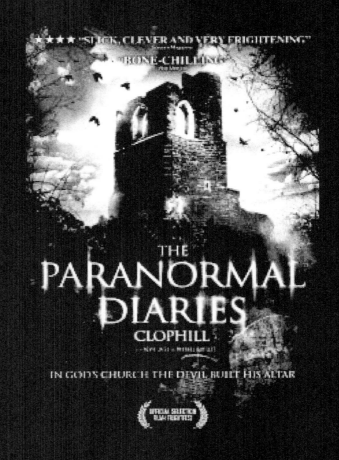

Kevin Gates' book and DVD movie.

Castle Cachtice

Tucked away in far northern Slovakia nestled in the Carpathian Mountains, overlooking a remote village lies the ruins of the castle belonging to one of the most notorious figures in history. Elizabeth Bathory was born in 1560 in Transylvania to a noble family. Her gruesome legacy continues to inspire films, books, music, plays and toys to this day. She was indeed the first noted female serial killer of all time.

She was obsessed with staying young and beautiful and would spend hours staring at herself in the mirror. She had a cruel, sadistic streak and also spent hours on coming up with new ways to inflict pain on enemies and soon began to practise on her servants. Legend has it that she once struck one of her servants drawing blood. A drop of blood splattered on her skin and she noticed the area of her skin where the blood had dropped was considerably clearer. This in turn developed her theory that bathing in human blood would restore her body to youthful appearance. She has allegedly have meant to have killed and bathed in the blood of up to 650 young girls.

She also had a gruesome interest in torture which, in turn, gave her sexual gratification. Some of her atrocities have said to have included burning with hot irons, mutilation of hands and faces, starving and sexual abuse. Rumours spread over Hungary of her gruesome activities and King Matthias sent soldiers to investigate. When they arrived at Cachtice they found the castle littered with corpses, some of them burned, some with no eyes, arms or legs. Bathory was put on house arrest straight away. Her subject accomplices were executed but she was spared the death sentence due to her nobility. She was imprisoned in a room of the castle with only a small hole to fit food and water where she remained until her death. She will be forever known as 'The Blood Countess'.

I visited Castle Cachtice in September 2016 and found it a remarkable place. To get there one has to catch a train from Bratislava to Nova Mesto Nad Vahom. From there you can get a connecting train to Cachtice Village. I would recommend getting a cab as it's a lengthy hike from the station to the village particularly if you have luggage. Or if you do as I did get off at the tiny neighbouring village of Visnove which the castle overlooks but is the wrong stop. I was fortunate enough to be able to communicate with one of the locals to give me a lift to Cachtice (very few people speak English in this neck of the woods) as the trains are very infrequent due to the remote location. A cab will only set you back around

I found Cachtice to be a charming friendly village and unbelievably cheap. Accommodation is available at Ubytovanie Apartments located in the centre of the village and can be booked online. Directly across the road is the village square where stands a huge statue of the Blood Countess. To get to the castle itself one simply has to follow the road from the village which leads directly to the castle. It's a steep climb and takes around 45 minutes depending on how fit you are. Once there you pay a small fee and are free to roam and explore for as long as you like. There's some breath-taking views of the Carpathians and the aforementioned village of Visnove. The tower where Bathory died is very much intact and in recent years the castle has undergone some much needed restoration. Some awesome little souvenirs are also available for purchase – which of course I did – including fridge magnets, postcards and a selection of Bathory blood red wines! There's even a Bathory Pizzeria in the village square where paintings of the Blood Countess adorn the walls.

No one really knows the full truth of Bathory's crimes but as they say there's no smoke without fire but I personally think the 600 victims is a gross exaggeration. The place is sparsely populated as it is let alone over four hundred years ago. However, if you have a keen sense of macabre history as I do then a trip to Cachtice comes highly recommended. I for one will be making a return visit at some stage.

View of Cachtice Castle from the village of Visnove.

View from Castle overlooking the village of Visnove.

The tower where Elizabeth Bathory was imprisoned and died.

Selection of Bathory wines.

Dungeon

The author next to a statue of the Blood Countess in Cachtice Village Square.

Some souvenirs bought by the author.

Mural on the wall of my accommodation.

Alcatraz

I know this may seem like an obvious choice being one of the world's most popular tourist destinations but ever since I saw the Clint Eastwood movie *Escape From Alcatraz* it has held a lifelong fascination for me. Most people are familiar with its history. The Rock as it's commonly known is a former United States military prison that was converted into a maximum security federal prison and opened on August 11, 1934. Its purpose was to house hardened troublesome prisoners and escapees from previous prisons with no hope of rehabilitation. A kind of 'last resort' prison. Some of its notorious inmates included Al Capone, George 'Machine Gun' Kelly, Franklin Stroud (the Birdman of Alcatraz) and James 'Whitey' Bulger.

Due to its location in the San Francisco Bay with its turbulent tides and freezing cold waters it was deemed escape proof. However on June 11, 1962 this was disproven. Inmates Frank Morris and brothers John and Clarence Anglin devised an intricate plan. This involved knocking out the grid in their cell walls, digging a hole large enough for them to fit through to an unused utility corridor, then up through a ventilation shaft and on to the roof. They then made their way down a fifty foot kitchen vent pipe and on to a blind spot from the search spotlight. Using a makeshift raft made from 50 stolen raincoats they made their way out on to the bay. They were never seen or heard from again.

The plan was masterminded by Frank Morris, who was known to have a superior I.Q. While plotting their escape they made dummy heads out of papier-mache and human hair from the prison barber shop. This gave the guards the impression they were sleeping in their beds. They also made replica wall grids out of cardboard to conceal the holes in their cell wall which also fooled the guards. The dummy heads were used the night of the escape so not to raise alarms and give them a head start. The prison authorities were quick to come to the conclusion that the men drown in the bay. However no bodies were ever found.

After discussing the escape with the tour guide who informed me that in fact many people had successfully swam across the bay when the tides were calm. And seeing the theory successfully put to the test on TV documentaries, such as *Mythbusters,* I personally think they made it. Particularly if Frank Morris had a thorough knowledge of the tide which he no doubt would have studied given his superior intelligence. It's highly unlikely they would have devised a meticulous plan like this and not taken into account getting across the bay to safety. But unless any of them come forward – which is highly unlikely as they're still wanted by the FBI - it will forever remain a mystery. The prison was closed on

March 21, 1963 as it cost three times the amount to run than normal prisons and the salt water had severely eroded the buildings.

Alcatraz is an absolute must whilst in San Francisco. It's a fifteen minute ferry ride across the bay which departs near Fisherman's Wharf. Once there you are given a recorded audio device which guides your journey from the point of view of the inmates. I was just happy to retrace Clint Eastwood's steps in the exercise yard and the Mess Hall. Other highlights were the infamous D-Block with its pitch black solitary confinement cells and of course the real Frank Morris' cell. This is now behind glass as it contains the original dummy head used in the escape tucked in the bed. The tour I went on was a package deal, it included three hours on Alcatraz, a stop at the Golden Gate Bridge and a full tour of the city. There are also night tours of the island which is definitely on the list on my next visit. Seeing the San Francisco skyline lit up from the island would be somewhat spectacular.

While there I also visited the spot where Church Of Satan founder Anton Lavey's Black House once stood. It's now just ugly condos that no one rents. San Francisco is a great town which again I hope to get back to in the not too distant future. Next time I hope to retrace the steps of the Zodiac Killer!

Exercise Yard

Frank Morris's cell with dummy head used in the escape.

Golden Gate Bridge in background.

The escapees, Frank Morris and the Anglin Bothers.

Auschwitz – Birkenau

Everyone knows what took place here, it's been documented in countless books, documentaries and films throughout the years. So for that reason I'm going to spare you the history lesson and just share my experiences of the place. The factory of death itself. They say no birds fly over this place. I'm not sure if that's exactly true or just another myth. I really wasn't looking out for any whilst I was there. But it really wouldn't surprise me. There are tours leaving from Krakow to Auschwitz on a daily basis. However because of their popularity I do advise you book in advance if you want a professional guided tour. Most companies will pick you up from your hotel and drop you back when the tour is finished. The tour I went on lasted around six hours.

There are two main camps to see – Auschwitz 1 Labour Camp and Auschwitz 11 – Birkenau Extermination Camp. They are located approximately 40 minutes from Krakow in the city of Oswiecim. The tour I went on showed a courtesy documentary film on the liberation of Auschwitz. The laughter from a group of jovial British tourists soon died down when the film began to play. Upon arrival you wait for your allocated tour guide in the administration block. The first thing you see when your tour begins is the famous 'Arbeit Macht Frei' (work brings freedom) sign above the entrance.

Though this is actually a replica as the original was stolen by a Swedish neo- Nazi who wanted to sell the sign to a wealthy collector and use the funds to organise terror campaigns. This never came to fruition however as the sign was found in a forest outside Gdansk and is currently in storage at the Auschwitz Birkenau Memorial Museum. From there you are taken on a guided tour of all the blocks. Everything about this place is truly grim, the smell, the bleak interior grey walls, the cold cement staircases, the photos of the victims adorning the walls, everything. Particularly if you go in November onwards as I did. It was a cold bleak day and it really suited the atmosphere of the place.

There you make your way around past the electrified fences until you come to the block containing the victims' belongings and two tons of human hair. These are behind glass and photographs are strictly forbidden. From there you come to the infamous Block 11, which was basically a prison within a prison. Prisoners were subjected to all kinds of heinous torture including the one square metre standing cells where up to four prisoners were forced to stand for up to twenty nights. There is also a dark chamber where inmates were confined without food or water and in between Block 10 and 11 is the infamous 'Death Wall' where executions by firing squad took place. From there you make your way to the far end of the camp to the guard tower where the morning role call took place to the first make shift gas chamber where the first experiments of Zyklon-B were carried out. Right next to this is the gallows where Camp Commandant Rudolf Hoss was hanged. This concludes the tour of Auschwitz 1. Most of what's here are reconstructions including the gallows so much of the materials that make up the camp aren't the originals from over seventy years ago. However, the reconstructions are a hundred percent accurate which makes for a very interesting yet harrowing experience. From there you board back on the bus for the short ten minute journey to Birkenau.

The first thing you see when you look out to the left is you're pulling into the carpark is the infamous 'Gate of Death' with its imposing guard tower and rail road running through the centre. As this was used primarily as an extermination camp apart from the iconic gate there really isn't that much here. Most of the barracks were dismantled after the war as they needed the materials. Once you pass the gate however you follow the tracks and come to the 'selection ramp'. This is where the arrivals were deemed fit or unfit for work. The latter were sent straight to the gas chamber upon arrival.

There is a wagon which was used for deportation and further down are the remains of the gas chambers which were blown up to destroy the evidence. There are a number of barracks still intact depicting the overcrowded wooden bunks and one with the latrines used for human waste. There are also memorial pools where human ash was dumped and several guard towers and fences but for the better part it's now mainly a big field surrounded by barbed wire fencing and guard towers. If you do the tour with a group you are permitted to enter the guard tower which gives you a bird's eye view of the whole camp. Overall a very important tour which really exposes you to the horrors mankind is capable of.

Guard tower where daily roll call took place.

The first gas chamber.

The infamous 'Gate Of Death' of Auschwitz – Birkenau.

The selection ramp where it was decided who was fit for work or straight to the gas chamber.

Destroying the evidence.

A pit where human ashes were dumped.

Transportation wagon.

A bunk where up to six inmates were crammed.

View inside Auschwitz – Birkenau from 'Gate Of Death' Tower.

Photo provided by publisher, common use

Hoia - Baciu Forest

The Hoia Baciu Forest is located in Transylvania just outside the city of Cluj Napoca. It has the reputation of being ranked in the top ten of the world's most haunted forests. And indeed is even referred to as the Bermuda Triangle of Romania. It has a reputation for intense paranormal activity and UFO sightings. The folkloric tales surrounding this place are incredible. One in particular involving a five year old girl who ventured into the forest and emerged five years later wearing the exact same clothing and hadn't aged one bit. The forest has a rotunda shaped clearing which has been described as a vegetation dead zone where no trees grow. Scientists have reportedly examined the soil and cannot draw a conclusion as to why this is the case. It is here where numerous UFO's have been caught on camera hovering above the rotunda. Including one taken by a military technician in the late 60's.

People entering the forest have experienced intense feelings of anxiety, nausea and the constant feeling of being watched. Electronic equipment is also known to mysteriously malfunction. Visitors have also witnessed ghostly apparitions, unexplained lights and the sounds of disembodied female laughter. The forest was named after a shepherd who entered the forest with his flock and never returned. The vegetation in the forest is also bizarre. It consists of weirdly shaped contorted trees with unexplained charring on the stumps and branches. The forest has also been said to be a portal to another dimension.

Hoia-Baciu as of course been the subject of several reality TV ghost hunts including *Ghost Adventures* whereupon crew members have become unexplicably physically ill. So, with a reputation like this how could I resist but to go and have a look for myself ? Tours can be booked online with the Hoia-Baciu Project. They will pick you up from your hotel or arrange to meet you at a location of your choice in Cluj Napoca. The drive to the forest takes around twenty minutes from Cluj and the tour lasts around three hours. My guide Alex was very helpful and had a thorough knowledge of the forest and its legendary history. I was the only one on this particular tour so that certainly helped to get a more detailed insight into the forest. You are provided with a bottle of water, a hiking stick and upon arrival make your way up a steep hill to the entrance of the forest. Our first stop was the infamous rotunda which is actually located near the entrance to the forest and not deep inside as some YouTube documentaries would have you believe. Campfires were still smouldering from the flight before from visitors no doubt hoping to catch a ghostly apparition or experience some sort of paranormal phenomena.

Well, it's certainly true, there are no trees growing in this particular area. Though I wouldn't go as far as to call it a vegetation dead zone. There are blades of long grass and weeds growing here. Alex answered all my questions with professional clarity. Some of what goes on here can be logically explained, other things cannot. He pointed out that whatever you experience in the forest all comes down to what sort of person you are. 'The forest picks up on your energy'. And I have to say this place certainly has a strong energy to it. But for me personally it gave me an overall calming effect. No feelings of nausea or anxiety here. We made our way through the forest and came across some of the weird looking contorted trees. I have to say I've never seen trees like this and they do look genuinely creepy. However, I'll take this opportunity to clear up a misconception. Upon googling the Hoia-Baciu images of serpentine looking pine trees bent at the base pop up on the screen. These are actually from a forest in Poland known as Crooked Forest and are NOT to be found in Hoia-Baciu. The story is someone added them to a website thus creating the deception. We made our way down one of the tracks and I have to say at this stage I got the feeling we were being followed and watched. Maybe it was my imagination, who knows?

That soon subsided however and the feeling of overall calm returned as we neared the end of the tour. Alex showed me shots of orbs and apparitions he'd captured on previous tours. The people in the photographs are oblivious to them as they weren't there when the pictures were taken. As we descended the hill back to the car we came across a herd of goats, which I found very appropriate! Overall though, for me a very pleasant experience. Apart from the aforementioned strange feeling nothing negative or unpleasant to speak of. Night tours are also available

Though there are many documentaries to be found on YouTube of the Hoia –Baciu many are misrepresentations and the footage of doubtful quality. *Hoia Baciu – Truth Or Legend?* is the first professionally produced documentary to date and will be available mid to late 2017 at time of writing. It will contain re-enactments of stories told by people who say they have experienced strange phenomena whilst visiting the forest as well as testimonies of Romanian and foreign tourists who have lived inexplicable moments, and interviews with various researchers.

Entrance to the forest.

The Clearing.

Twisted looking trees in the forest.

A herd of goats on the outskirts of the forest.

Classic photo of the alleged Loch Ness monster, "Nessie," provided by publisher, common use

Loch Ness

It was always a childhood dream of mine to visit this vast mysterious stretch of water located in the Scottish Highlands. From a very young age I was fascinated by the legend of the Loch Ness Monster. I'd read every book that was in the school library, watch every documentary, talk about it with friends. I used to fantasise about being part of a search party seeking out the elusive beast. It's this very phenomenon that has spawned countless documentaries, big budget Hollywood productions and has intrigued explorers, scientists, journalists and curiosity seekers for decades.

At twenty four miles in length and nearly two miles in width it's Britain's largest body of fresh water. Eight hundred feet deep in parts it's enough to immerse every man woman and child on the planet five times over. Certainly enough room for its fair share of mysteries. You can paddle out from the shore in parts as far as twelve feet before hitting a sudden drop plunging into the black abyss. Other parts particularly near Urquhart Castle there is no shallow water. Just a straight drop off the shore into the depths.

Over the years there have been countless numbers of sightings, photographs and sonar scans of the beast that supposedly inhabits these murky waters. Some from very reputable members of the community including police officers, hotel managers and priests. My dreams came to fruition in 2008, 2011 and again in 2016. It was everything I expected and more. Every bit as vast and imposing as what they say! Stretching for miles as far as the eye can see. Beautiful and sombre yet dark and intimidating. One could truly imagine this being the lair of H.P. Lovecraft's sea monster Cthulhu.

George Edwards is Skipper of Loch Ness cruise boat the Nessie Hunter. He has been hunting the elusive creature for over twenty six years and is the longest serving passenger boat skipper on Loch Ness. In 1987 he recorded the greatest known depth of Loch Ness at 812 feet which was subsequently named after him – 'Edwards Deep' I was fortunate to take a trip on one of his cruises on my 2011 visit and discovered that he was a true believer in these creatures emphasising that there's 'no smoke without fire'. Of course he has had numerous sightings over the years and indeed has photographic evidence of his sightings in the form of postcards which he sells on his boat. However, there are sceptics who doubt the credibility of his photographs some calling him a faker. Though one could almost forgive him if this was the case. After all the mystery is what keeps the legend alive and the tourism industry thriving in Loch Ness. You kill the legend, you kill the attraction, simple as that.

Cruise Loch Ness is another service which departs from Fort Augustus at the southern end of the Loch. One of the skippers on the boat the Royal Scott has had multiple sightings over the years and apparently very credible evidence. Including sonar footage of something around thirty foot long moving in the depths and photographs of what appear to be carcasses of unidentified creatures. His nickname is 'Ricky the Monster Man'. I paid a visit to Fort Augustus on two occasions with the intention of having a chat with him about it and hopefully even maybe letting me see some of this footage. The first time it was his day off and the second time he was on holidays – bloody typical!

To date I have visited the Loch three times and have yet to catch a glimpse of the beast that is said to inhabit its murky depths. Because of its natural terrain it is impossible to walk around the entire perimeter of the Loch's shores. I know of three locations where one can access the shores. One involves a walk through Urquhart Woods in the village of Drumnadrochit, Fort Augustus provides probably the best view from its lookout point which is accessible via a path alongside the Caledonian Canal leading up to the mouth of the Loch stretching as far as the eye can see. The other is on Dores Beach heading towards Inverness. It is also here that you will find full time Nessie Hunter, Steve Feltham. Parked permanently in his old mobile library home since 1991 with no electricity or running water he has dedicated most of his life searching for the elusive beast. With the only funding coming from the sales of his hand made Nessie models. To say the man is dedicated is a gross understatement.

On all of my visits I've stayed at the charming Morlea On Green, Bed & Breakfast. Located in the centre of the picturesque village of Drumnadrochit within walking distance to the shores of the Loch via Urquhart Woods. The village has two exhibitions and a couple of life size statues of Nessie as well as numerous gift and souvenir shops. The Morlea is run by an English couple, Laurence and Tracey. They are lovely people and very hospitable. In the winter months Laurence supplements the guest income by chimney sweeping. He told me of a certain house he was sweeping on the east side of the Loch. Once owned by one of the most notorious figures in history. This provided another theory on the Loch Ness Monster. One that could explain its elusiveness. Which brings us to our next segment.

A night time view of Urquhart Castle.

Nessie Hunter Steve Feltham's converted mobile library home. He's been camped here for the better part of thirty years and as yet to catch a glimpse of the elusive beast.

Urquhart Castle from the Nessie Hunter boat.

Sombre view of the Loch from Fort Augustus.

𝔅𝔬𝔩𝔢𝔰𝔨𝔦𝔫𝔢 𝔥𝔬𝔲𝔰𝔢

Boleskine House is located on the south-east shores of Loch Ness a mile north of the tiny village of Foyers. It is best known for being the former residence one of the most notorious figures in history. A man whom the British press dubbed 'The Most Wickedest Man in the World', 'The Great Beast 666' - occult mystic, Aleister Crowley. Crowley was born into a wealthy Plymouth Brethren family but renounced his fundamentalist Christian faith bestowed upon him by his family when he reached adolescence whilst studying at the University of Cambridge. He eventually inherited a family fortune which enabled him to pursue Western Esotericism and a life of hedonistic indulgence and decadence. He joined the London based Hermetic Order of the Golden Dawn – an esoteric order comprising of some very influential members of society including *Dracula* author Bram Stoker. Here he was trained in ceremonial magic before splitting from the order embarking on his own path.

Crowley purchased Boleskine House in 1899 for the sole purpose of performing an epic magical ceremony called the 'Abremalin Operation', an angel summoning ritual that requires a secluded place and months of meditation and abstinence. The purpose of the ritual is to obtain the knowledge and conversation of the magician's Holy Guardian Angel. Once the preparation phase is complete the guardian angel will allegedly appear and reveal magical secrets. The magician is then to invoke the twelve kings and dukes of hell and bind them. Thereby gaining control over them in his own mental universe.

"I picked Boleskine for its loneliness, the perfect location to perform this operation". Crowley is reported to have said. However things didn't quite transpire as Aleister had planned. For whatever reason he abandoned the operation altogether before completing it. Maybe he grew impatient or got sick of living a monk's lifestyle of abstinence being the hedonistic individual he was. Who knows? This apparently resulted in the summoning of bad demons beyond his control – or so the story goes. Thus, to this day, many locals stay well clear of the place.

Crowley remained at Boleskine House until 1913 with many sinister goings on reported to have taken place, including his house keeper going out of his mind and attempting to kill Crowley before disappearing completely. A local butcher allegedly cut off his own hand when he received an order of meat from Crowley with a spell written on the other side of the paper. Shadowy figures were also seen around the house and property. Legend has it that a church once stood on the site of the house which consequently caught fire and burned to the ground, roasting the entire congregation along with it. A story which Crowley reportedly took delight in propagating. Indeed, sinister activity in the form of ghostly apparitions in the adjacent Boleskine Cemetery pre-dates his arrival. Bad luck and tragedies would plague subsequent owners after his departure.

In 1971 the estate was purchased by Led Zeppelin guitarist and Crowley enthusiast Jimmy Page, who reportedly had the world's largest Crowley book collection and other personal belongings of the mystic. Though Page only spent a total of six weeks at the house in the entirety of his ownership. He left it in the care of his long term friend Malcolm Dent who lived there with his family. Dent experienced a series of sinister goings on whilst caretaker there, including unexplained rearranged furniture, gale force winds whilst perfectly still outside, a dark presence shrouding the house in total darkness in broad daylight and a shadowy figure trying to get under the door of his bedroom.

Page sold Boleskine in 1992 which has since been resold and is now in private ownership. The current owners have since changed the name of the estate and want to eradicate all previous history and reputation surrounding the house in an attempt to reinvent it as a normal respectable residence. Good luck with that, I say! Like the ruins of Clophill Church they could turn it into a thriving, lucrative business by transforming it into a museum dedicated to the Great Beast himself. Needless to say

Crowley enthusiasts are certainly not welcome to rock up and roam around the property. Trespassing is illegal and you have to respect the owners right to privacy.

Though one is totally free to roam around Boleskine Cemetery. There's reportedly an underground passage leading from the house to a stone hut in the far corner of the cemetery across the road. Rumour has it that this is an old embalming room. The interior is adorned with Crowley related graffiti including the iconic 'Do What Thou Wilt', as well as a supply of empty beer cans. Tell-tale signs of thrill seeking Crowleyites!

I visited the site in 2011. I got as close to the house as I possibly could from the paddock next door. The house itself is far from sinister in its appearance. It's a modest low set home painted white with neatly trimmed shrubs, it sits on top of a hill with a spectacular view overlooking Loch Ness. Truly magnificent, it looks like an idyllic country retreat, a welcoming B&B. Which indeed it has been. I wandered around the cemetery for a couple of hours taking in the atmosphere and history of the place. I have to say the energy was quite eerie but also beautiful and tranquil. This was in the middle of the afternoon however. I imagine visiting the site under the cover of total darkness would be quite an unnerving experience.

Though it's only fitting that the so called 'Great Beast' would choose such a location for this special purpose. An isolated house on the shores of a vast lake supposedly inhabited by a Leviathan type sea monster. Indeed one of the theories is that Nessie isn't actually a physical creature. Rather a spiritual one summoned from a portal to another dimension by Crowley himself! This could explain the sheer volume of sightings yet no concrete physical evidence after decades of meticulous research. Or so the story goes! An unfortunate accident occurred just before Christmas

2015 whereupon a raging fire gutted the place destroying sixty percent of the iconic mansion. The fire is said to have been caused by a spin dryer and not deliberate. I visited the house again in 2016 to see what remained. The place just stands there unattended and one is easily able to roam around inside of the remains as I did. The future of it is uncertain. Whether the current owners intend to level it and start again is unclear. Perhaps a wealthy Crowley devotee will restore it and turn it into a lucrative museum? Time will tell.

I did attempt to visit Crowley's other abode – The Abbey Of Thelema in Cefalu , Sicily in 2017. Crowley relocated here in 1920 with some of his followers with the aim of setting up an idealistic utopia. A school of magic for students to indulge in ritual practices. To discover the great work of manifesting their true will.

Italian fascist dictator Benito Mussolini didn't like the idea of a magic practicing decadent commune on his soil. Therefore, ordered Crowley to leave the country in 1923. The villa still stands today but is so dilapidated and run down that a fence has been erected around the perimeter of the property with signs warning - 'Private Property' and 'No Trespassing'. The murals Crowley painted on the walls have long since faded and the place is in such disrepair that it isn't safe to venture inside. Though I was keen to check it out for myself I got as far as the nearby city of Palermo when something went horribly pear shaped preventing me from continuing with my journey and had to return. Maybe next time.

Boleskine Cemetery.

former embalming room. Rumour has it there was a tu
leading from the house to the room.

he remains of Boleskine House after it was gutted by fir

Externsteine

Ranging from 20 to 38 meters in height these thirteen rocks located in the Teutoburg Forest just outside the town of Horn – Bad Meinberg in north-west Germany make up the striking natural monument that is Externsteine. This sandstone ancient rock structure is said to have been formed from an eruption around 70 million years ago. Its history prior to the 12th century remains a mystery. Throughout its history it has said to have been an ancient Germanic cult site used as a Heathen- Saxon sanctuary but was also used by early Christians as a place of worship. Indeed there is a carving the body of Christ, Mary, a bearded dragon and Adam and Eve. This was carved out in 1130 by Paderborn Benedictine monks. There is also a chapel with an altar and a window opening at the top of rock 2 which is only accessible by climbing the stairway on rock 3 and crossing an arched bridge at the peak. On the 21st of June – the Summer Solstice - the rising sun shines through the round opening over the altar. There is also a Grotto with three chambers connected by a passageway located at the base of the structure on the inside of the rocks. Above the entrance to the main chamber is a carving of a winged creature indicating a possible temple for ancient pagan worship. This is unfortunately not open to the public for reasons of monument maintenance.

The Nazis used the stones as a focus of nationalistic propaganda, with a section of the SS conducting studies for Germanic folklore and history. Because Externsteine has a reputation of being a sacred pagan site it became a popular pilgrimage spot on the Summer Solstice and Walpurgisnacht from the 1980's to late 2000's. However, numbers began to excel to that of around 3,500 so the Municipalities of Lippe put a stop to this by prohibiting camping, open fires and alcohol consumption. Not because of the nature of the occasions but as a concern for binge drinking and potential vandalism to the site which is understandable.

I visited what is often referred to as the 'Germanic Stonehenge' on the Summer Solstice of 2016 and I have to say it really is a site to behold. The structure is best accessed from the cities of either Detmold or Horn-Bad Meinberg. I was staying in the latter – a charming peaceful town with beautiful surroundings. A short bus ride took me straight to it. It's around a ten minute walk from the main road up a path. Simply follow the signs. You get to the visitor centre, go past the restaurant and the rocks are just a bit further down the track. You pay a small fee of 4 euros and this allows you to climb the structure and spend as long as you'd like

Climbing the stairway can be a bit laborious but once you get to the top at the arch bridge the views are simply magnificent. You can also walk right up to the upper chapel and altar via the bridge. A walk around the lake to the right of the structure is very serene and you can grab some fantastic photos from this angle. There is also a road running between to the structure where you can access the other side. A tramline was once here running from Detmold to Paderborn but was closed in 1953. It truly is a magical, mystical site in which I hope to return in the not too distant future.

ar at the top of main rock. On the Summer Solstice the
shines straight through the window.

Statuary art created by the Paderborn monks.

Castle Wewelsburg

Wewelsburg is a renaissance castle located in the district of Buren, Westphalia not far from the city of Paderborn. It is a triangular structure with three round towers connected by massive walls. It was here that SS Chief Heinrich Himmler set out to create an embodiment of mystical power. An ideological centre and refuge for the SS elite that after the final victory of the Third Reich would become the spiritual centre of the world.

In 1934 Himmler signed a 100 year lease to take over the fortress to create a Germanic leadership school for the SS. A Nazi Vatican you might say. A concentration camp was set up on the grounds next to the castle whereupon the inmates began redesigning the castle to Himmler's satisfaction as forced labour. He designed the rooms and named them after military heroes such as King Arthur, King Henry the Lion, Widikund and Frederick the Great. Walls were decorated with swastikas, ancient Germanic runes and other mystical symbols. Even tableware and cutlery were adorned with SS logos. He assembled twelve SS officers who were in effect his knights of the round table. They engaged in occult rites in celebration with the national socialist state. It was also used as an operation centre where Himmler and his officers plotted the occupation of Eastern Europe and invasion of the USSR.

The two main rooms were in the North Tower. The cellar got converted to what is known as the 'Crypt'. This was to be used as a chamber for solemn death rituals. A pit was designed in the centre of the room where an eternal flame was to burn to honour the dead. A swastika rune adorned the ceiling directly above. The room above the north tower was the SS General's Hall or 'Obergruppenfuhrersaal'. It was designed with twelve pillars around the perimeter of the room with a marble mosaic pagan sun wheel in the centre of the floor. When it became apparent that there was going to be no final victory and Germany would be defeated Himmler had the castle destroyed with explosives and tank mines.

Restoration began in 1948 and in 1950 it became a museum and youth centre. In 2010 it underwent a £5 million revamp and reopened as 'The Ideology and Terror of the SS' exhibition. Some critics have labelled it 'Naziland'. However, the curators are adamant that the idea is to provide an education on how quickly a civilised state can collapse into depravity and mass murder. I visited the museum in June 2016. The best way to get there is catch a 460 bus from the bus station to the left of Paderborn station when you reach the village of Wewelsburg get off at the Kreismuseum/ Skule stop. Just look for the school. Now unless you know what to look for it can be quite tricky as the castle is quite well hidden from the street. From the school walk up, then down the hill, then up again, you'll see a path on the right heading down beside a youth hostel. Follow that and it brings you straight to the castle. Try not to do as I did and get a cab from Paderborn. I was waiting around for the bus which didn't show. I wasn't sure if I'd missed it or it was running late and I was limited for time. It set me back 40 euros and you don't want that.

You'll see a building adjacent to the castle. This is the building for the exhibition. It's also free off charge so it's definitely worth a look. There's also a souvenir shop with a great selection of books, fridge magnets and postcards etc. You go down the stairs and the exhibition begins. Basically, it's a chronological progression of the SS, documenting social structure and organisation. It's made of glass display cabinets with some very interesting authentic items. These include – photos, helmets, daggers, uniforms, journals and much more. There's a lot to see so allow yourself 90 mins to 2 hours to get round the whole thing. From there you get access to the north tower with the Crypt and SS Generals Hall. I was warned that photos are strictly forbidden in both rooms so I duly respected their wishes. The Crypt was everything I expected - a big desolate medieval looking chamber that echoed every footstep. The pit of the eternal flame lies dead centre with the rune swastika directly above on the ceiling, although there are now paintings adorning the circumference of the chamber commemorating the victims.

Directly upstairs is the Obergruppenfuhrersaal , and the bit about the no photos was probably just as well here. The marble mosaic of the sun wheel was covered in orange bean bags, why? This didn't make sense and completely ruined it. I did consider moving them and grabbing a photo as I was the only one in the room but it was probably under surveillance and I didn't want to risk a fine or having my camera confiscated. The conclusion to the exhibition is a model of the concentration camp and the testimony of some of the survivors. Overall a fascinating visit and an absolute must for any World War 2 enthusiast. The other towers of the castle contain museums of its other medieval history but it was near closing time. And I didn't want another 40 euro cab fare.

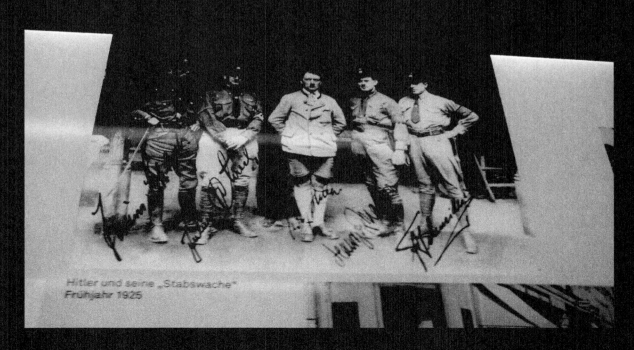

Hitler und seine „Stabswache"
Frühjahr 1925

SS uniform in the 'Fascination and Terror' Exhibition

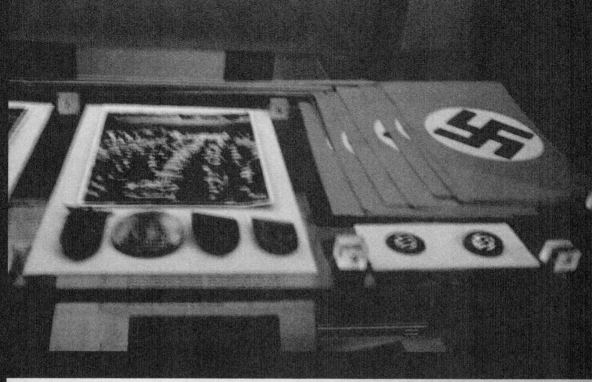

Castle Houska

Many of the world's alleged dark places are nothing more than historically mythical locations constructed purely of spooky urban legends. However, Castle Houska located 47 kilometres north of Prague in the Czech Republic has a far more sinister history to it. It is said to have been constructed over a bottomless pit which is a gateway to Hell itself. Half animal human hybrids are said to have crawled out of the pit preying on local villagers and livestock. Dark winged other worldly creatures were also seen flying in the vicinity.

The castle has no exterior fortification, water sources or trade fare routes. There were also no occupants upon construction so technically there's no real reason for it to exist. In fact, all the defence fortifications seemed to be on the interior. Specifically designed to keep something in, not out. So it wasn't designed as a residence or protective sanctuary but to seal the pit and keep these hellish creatures trapped below the ground. Whilst the castle was being built inmates who were sentenced to death were offered a pardon if they volunteered to be lowered into the pit and report back what they saw. The first of these volunteers was said to have been a young man. He was slowly lowered into the pit until he disappeared out of sight whereupon there remained a silence. Shortly thereafter maniacal, hysterical screaming could be heard coming from the depths of the pit. When he was brought back up he had clearly aged around thirty years. He had grown wrinkles and his hair had turned pure white. He couldn't report what he had saw as he had gone completely mad and died in an asylum two days later of unknown causes.

Throughout its history the castle has been occupied by various individuals seeking to use the castle's evil power for their own personal gain. One of these was the Commander of the Swedish Army during the 30 years war. Commander Oronto was said to be a practitioner of black magic and wanted to achieve immortality. This of course never came to be as he was shot by two local hunters through a window. The Nazis also occupied the castle briefly in the late 1930's. They were said to have conducted experimental physics in an attempt to harness the powers of Hell for themselves. There was nothing strategically to be gained by the Nazis occupying Houska. There was nothing of any importance in that region. Evidently it didn't end well for them either as the bodies of SS soldiers were found in the courtyard. They had all been executed. But by who? The current owners won't allow any excavation to prove if there really is a hell beneath the castle for fear of unexploded mines left by the occupying Nazis.

I recently visited Houska at the time of writing. It was the last place on the list for this project. If you're looking to visit here by public transport forget it. This is northern Bohemia and really is in the middle of nowhere. A friend drove me from the town of Velke Porici north east of Prague near the Polish border and it took us just on two hours. However, there is a company in Prague – McGee's Ghost Tours - who will drive you there and back. Which is probably the easiest option if you're travelling, limited for time and don't want to hire out a car. It is very accessible from Prague and can easily be done within an afternoon.

The drive through the Bohemian countryside is truly beautiful. You pass many pine forests and other castles along the way. As you're approaching you make your way up a long winding road which is shaded by a thick forest on either side. Even in the mid afternoon sun everything seems to go dark and certainly adds to the creepy atmosphere of your destination. Finally the square gothic stone structure is visible through the thick forest. You are met with a cool looking sign of a demon turning the handle of a meat grinder in the shape of Houska as you enter the car park!

From the car park you make your way up a country path (not unlike that of Castle Cachtice I might add) about three hundred meters past an old looking wooden chapel and some cool looking structures built within the rocks until you arrive at the main gates on your right. And you are here – The Gateway To Hell.

The first thing you notice is how many windows there are on the outside walls. However, interestingly enough, many of these are fake with nothing behind them but solid walls. It was a Sunday afternoon when we went and inside the ground were various stalls and markets selling all sorts of cool little Bohemian artefacts. Some stall owners adorned costumes with devil's horns which certainly added to the festive atmosphere. Tickets are purchased at the little souvenir shop to the right of the main gates. We arrived just in the nick of time for the allocated tour at 4pm. The guide was dressed in Bohemian monk robes and of course didn't conduct the tour in English. Therefore, I had to follow a written English translation the best I could. The tour commenced in the interior courtyard where he explained the origins and its conversion during the renaissance period. We then made our way up the interior staircase to the hunting room. I've never seen so many hunting trophies in my life - deer, ram, bear, wild boar, and birds. One wall was adorned entirely with ram's heads!

From there we went up into the knight's drawing room which had various coats of arms of the wall and weapons and armour on display. From there it was up to the dining room on the top floor which provided some breath taking views of the surrounding countryside. The guide gave another talk on the top floor interior balcony and it was time to head back down to the ground floor on to the chapel.

The chapel is the oldest part of the castle and legend has it was built over the top of the crack in the earth to the bottomless pit to act as a weight to keep the hellish creatures underground. They had previously tried to fill it with stones but the hole was so deep it just swallowed all attempts to fill it.

The chapel walls are adorned with ancient frescoes. One of Arch Angel Michael fighting a dragon which was symbolic of evil. One however depicts an half animal half human female creature drawing a bow at another human. She is using her left hand to draw the bow which back then was symbolic of Satan. Perhaps this is a representation of some of the creatures that were meant to inhabit the pit below?

Finally, it was to see Hell itself. Next door is a dark underground cavern known as 'Satan's Office'. This is what I'd come to see! This really has the feeling of a true Satanic Temple. You go down the first flight of rickety stairs, iron sculptures of demon's heads hang from the ceiling and on the walls. Then down the second flight of stairs into Satan's lair. A throne sits at the back centre with glowing cauldrons either side. This really would be the perfect location for a Satanic ritual. On this occasion there were two actors, one demon looking guy with horned top hat welcoming people to Hell and one sitting on the throne who I presumed to be the Devil. Though in all seriousness he looked more like Johnny Depp's character Jack Sparrow than the Devil!

As well as being the Gateway To Hell, Castle Houska of course is also renowned for being one of the most haunted locations in the Czech Republic. A ghost of a beautiful blonde woman wearing a long white dress is said to wander the third floor, a headless corpse is said to wander the courtyard with blood gushing from its neck and a faceless black robed priest is said to haunt Satan's Office. There's been various reports of people hearing screams and moans from below the surface and witnessing shadowy apparitions. The current owner, Jaromir Simonek, was having drinks with friends on the third floor when he witnessed his glass levitate in the air then slide to the middle of the table.

It was a bright sunny afternoon when I visited and there were a lot of tourists. Certainly more than I expected and I have to say it certainly did detract from its sinister reputation. However, I was to learn that Czech people embrace dark folklore as part of their culture. Which I have to say is a welcome change from dismissing it as pure nonsense. Given the right atmosphere and surroundings however I'm certain this place could be truly chilling.

Devilish décor in 'Satan's Office'.

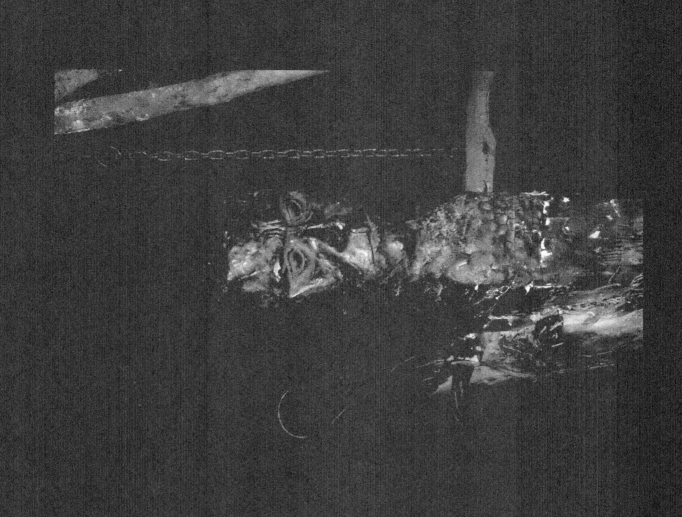

Welcoming sign with the Devil and Houska as a meat grinder.

Nazi Party Rally Grounds – Nuremberg

These were the locations used for six rallies in the south east of Nuremberg that were held between 1933 – 1938 and were featured in the Nazi propaganda film *Triumph Of The Will*. Though they weren't rallies as such, they were more like showcase parades as a demonstration of power to boost Nazi morale. The best way to get to the sites is catch a number 10 bus from the main square of Old Town Nuremberg to the Dokumentationszentrum Reichsparteitagselande (Documentation Centre Nazi Party Rally Grounds) which is the last stop on the route. This is the Congress Hall building. It was inspired by the Roman Coliseum in design and is the largest preserved national socialist building. It was initially designed to seat 50,000 people but was never completed. A roof was never attached therefore the building is in the shape of a gigantic 'U'.

Upon arrival it is best to venture around the building past the picturesque lake to see the grounds themselves. From the lake you make your way up the Great Road, originally designed by Nazi architect Albert Speer as a military parade ground for the Wehrmacht. There are plaques on posts depicting its history, however to read them I suggest you brush up on your German. From there you walk through the picturesque surroundings until you come to what remains of the flag stations surrounding Zeppelin Field. You keep walking until you come to what's left on the grandstand known as the Zeppelintribune surrounded either side by dilapidated weed covered stairs. This is where Hitler stood in his podium and where the masses witnessed their Fuhrer's finest performances. This is also where the US army blew up the swastika which adorned the top of the Zeppelin Tribune building as a symbolic gesture of victory. The site is now nothing more than a crumbling shell of its former glory.

Gone are the pillared structures either side of the main building. They were demolished after the war being deemed unsafe and in disrepair. There is even a sign warning 'Enter At Your Own Risk' but there are still plaques adorning the decaying walls depicting how it once looked. The podium where the Fuhrer once stood overlooking the field still remains – or so we are led to believe but it's not the original. Needless to say thousands of visitors each year take selfies doing their best Fuhrer impressions. Though it's still an interesting site to visit when you think what took place here. The 'Cathedral Of Light' involved the use of 152 anti-aircraft search lights. The spectacle was designed by Albert Speer to give the effect of vertical beams of light shooting into the night sky above the Zeppelintribune. It was a spectacular sight and apparently could be seen from as far away as Prague. The field itself is now half car park and is used for sporting events, motor racing and open air concerts on occasions.

After a lengthy wander around Zeppelin Field I made my way back to the Congress Hall building to check out the 'Fascination and Terror' Museum located in the northern wing of the building. It is a thoroughly documented museum chronicling the rise and fall of the Third Reich in its entirety. Complete with audio commentary through headphones at each exhibit station as well as film footage, photos and exhibits I suggest you allow yourself 2-3 hours to get around it and take it all in. At the conclusion of the museum you are entitled to a full view of the interior courtyard of the building via an extended platform. It provides a great view and is a good opportunity to grab some photos.

My only regret is not visiting the former Luitpold Arena which unbeknownst to me at the time is located directly across the road from the Documentation Centre. This is where the Nazi Party held there 'Cult of the Dead' rally as a commemoration of the fallen in World War 1.Where the iconic footage of Adolf Hitler, SS leader Heinrich Himmler, and SA leader Viktor Lutze are seen walking the lengthy path towards the Ehrenhalle - Hall of Honour - before giving the Nazi salute, flanked either side by thousands of Stormtroopers. Upon research the site is totally unrecognizable to its days of glory. All the Nazi structures have been demolished and it has been converted into parklands. The only thing that remains is what's left of the Ehrenhalle, the granite path leading up to it and the six pillars either side that contained fire bowls at the rallies. Still, visiting this would have topped off a what was a fine day of history.

Alter Tiergarten

Ehemaliges
Reichsparteitags-
gelände

GESAMTPLAN

Plan des Reichsparteitagsgeländes
(Postkarte 1937).

In seinem Konzept für das Reichsparteitagsgelände hob Architekt Albert Speer den Anfang der Großen Straße mit zwei großen Türmen hervor. Gegenüber der Kongresshalle waren ein „Bau für die Kulturtagungen" und ein „Ausstellungsbau" vorgesehen. Diesen Plänen stand der Tiergarten im Weg. Die Nationalsozialisten ließen ihn deshalb 1939 an den heutigen Standort am Schmausenbuck im Osten Nürnbergs verlegen.

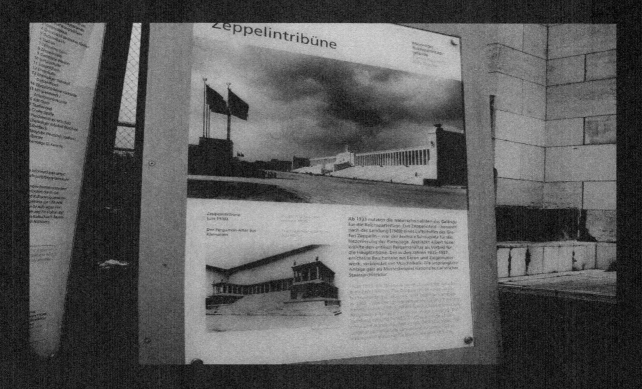

The Zeppelin Tribune in its former glory.

Now just a dilapidated shell.

Interior of the Congress Hall Building.

The Fuhrer's supposed former podium, Zeppelin Field.

Poenari Fortress – The Real Castle Dracula

Whenever Castle Dracula comes to mind one usually conjures up images of a gothic monolith perched on top of a mountain overlooking a Transylvanian Valley. Indeed, this is the case with Bran Castle located in Romania on the Transylvanian/Wallachian border. Bram Stoker based the castle in his iconic novel on Bran Castle after seeing a sketch of it. However the historical figure on which Stoker based his character Count Dracula on had no real association with this castle. It is thought that he may have stayed there from time to time and fought some battles in the region but that's as far as it goes.

The real Castle Dracula has an idyllic location very similar to that depicted in the novel and is former residence to one of the most brutal, bloodthirsty figures in history – Vlad Tepes. Commonly known as Vlad The Impaler. So named for his cruel method of impaling his enemies alive on wooden stakes. He was Prince of Wallachia and ruled the region three times between 1448 and his death in 1476. He also defended the region from Sultan Mehmed II and the Ottoman Empire.

Though there are several companies that do tours to the Poenari Fortress the one I went on was through a company called Travel Maker. This tour stopped in the city of Targoviste where the ruins of the Princely Court are located. This was also a fortress of Vlad's who built an observation tower there. The tower is still fully intact and you are able to climb the interior spiral staircase providing you with a panoramic view of Targoviste from the top. It was here that Sultan Mehmed II and his army walked into what he described as a 'Forest of the Impaled'. Thousands of men women and children spitted like pigs. He was both amazed and dumbfounded at what he saw. Stating that it was not possible to deprive a country of a man capable of such diabolical deeds and promptly turned back.

Poenari Fortress itself is literally located in the middle of nowhere, on the plateau of Mount Cetatea. At the foot of it lies the Arges River and legend has it that when the fortress was besieged by an Ottoman army led by Vlad's brother, 'Handsome Radu', Vlad's wife threw herself from the fortress into the river below rather than be taken captive by the Ottomans. Though how much truth is in this is anyone's guess. This tale inspired Arges to be named the 'Lady River' in folklore. Once there one has the daunting task of climbing 1,470 stairs to get to the fortress. The climb takes approximately half an hour – depending on one's physical fitness. At the top you pay a small fee and are free to explore the fortress for as long as you like. There are a couple of props including two impaled wax dummies, gallows and torture rack.

The panoramic views of the surrounding areas and valley are simply breath taking and well worth the climb. The fortress itself is small compared with Elizabeth Bathory's Castle Cachtice and can be seen within twenty minutes. There really isn't a lot left apart from the surrounding fortified walls and the remains of a tower still relatively intact. But if you have any interest in Vlad the Impaler it's well worth a visit. Of course at the start of the entrance there are tiny stalls selling fridge magnets and figurines, etc, so you can grab yourself a Vlad souvenir to conclude your descent!

Just up the road is also the Vindraru Dam. The company I went with included this on the tour and it's definitely worth a look whilst you're in the area. It's a breath-taking 166 meters high and also features a metal statue of Prometheus overlooking the lake/dam.

Travel Maker also offers tours to Vlad's birthplace. A three-storey mustard coloured building in the town of Sighisoara. The ground floor serves as a restaurant whereas the actual room where Vlad was born features a coffin in which someone dressed as Dracula jumps out and scares the wits out of unsuspecting visitors. A bust sculpture of Vlad is located in the village square. His final resting place is said to be in Snagov Monastery – a 14th century monastery in the middle of Snagov Lake. Though most historians are adamant that this tomb is empty and his true resting place unknown.

ervation tower at Targoviste Fortress built by Vlad ?paler and Poenari Fortress high above on the summ

The author at the entrance to the castle.

Impaled props.

View from the fortress.

Souvenirs bought by the author.

Vindraru Dam not far from Poenari Fortress.

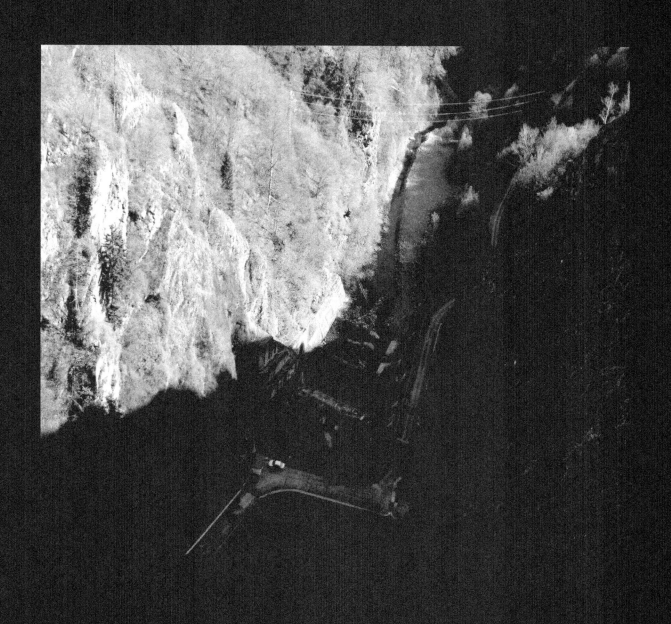

Pendle Hill

Located in Lancashire England Pendle Hill is a brooding presence 557 meters high at its peak towering above local villages and hamlets it can be seen from miles away. This area is best known for the Pendle Witch Trials which took place in 1612 which saw ten people convicted and hanged for witchcraft. You could say it was the UK's equivalent of the Salem Witch Trials though this took place some eighty years earlier. The main characters were two feuding peasant matriarchs – Elizabeth Southern known as 'Old Demdike' and Anne Whittle known as 'Old Chattox'. Both women were feared in the local god-fearing superstitious community. It was a time of religious persecution and intolerance. King

James I had survived the gunpowder plot by Guy Fawkes and his suspicious nature led to an obsession with witchcraft. Catholics were also demonised.

The hysteria started on March 18, 1612 when Alizon Device, the granddaughter of Old Demdike was begging on a road to the town of Colne. She asked a passing pedlar for some pins who in turn refused. She allegedly cursed him whereupon a huge black dog appeared. She ordered it to lame the pedlar who then collapsed being paralysed down the left side. He more than likely suffered what's commonly known as a stroke. She was hauled before the Justice Roger Nowell where she confessed to witchcraft and was forced to give an account of her and the Chattox family's malevolent activities. Nowell then ordered Demdike, Chattox, and her daughter Anne Redfearn to give evidence on the evil deeds they'd done to the local community. Demdike confessed claiming that the Devil came to her in a local quarry in the shape of a little boy called Tibb who had sucked her blood leaving her stark mad. The three women were then sent to Lancaster Castle to be put on trial for witchcraft.

Truth be known the women were more than likely products of their own imaginations which had convinced themselves of having supernatural powers. What else did they have in their lives besides poverty and little to no prospects? Shortly thereafter twenty people gathered on Good Friday at Demdike's home, a cottage known as Malkin Tower. This was thought to be a Sabbat where they feasted on a stolen sheep and planned to blow up Lancaster Castle, kill the keeper Thomas Cowell and free the imprisoned women. An investigator was sent to Malkin Tower where unearthed human bones were found along with a clay figure used to cause the ceremonial destruction of their enemies. Three people present at the gathering were sent for questioning where one, James Device, confessed to the lingering death of local woman Anne Towneley by slowly crumbling the clay image of her. Demdike's grand-daughter, Jennie Device, named all the people at the gathering who were then rounded up and sent to join the other supposed witches at Lancaster Castle.

The trial was a farce. The accused had no legal counsel or defence lawyer and the only prosecuting witness was nine year old Jennet Device who gave evidence against her own family and other villagers. However, they were all found guilty of witchcraft. So on August 20, 1612 Chattox, Anne Redfearn, Elizabeth, James and Alizon Device, Alice Nutter, Katherine Hewitt, and Jane and John Bulcock were all hanged on a hill above Lancaster Castle. Demdike died in the castle dungeon whilst awaiting trial.

Pendle Hill is still a hot spot on Halloween with hundreds of people making the pilgrimage every year dressed in their best Halloween garb. And to honour those unjustly executed, on the 400th anniversary of the trial the year 1612 was etched in huge numbers on the hillside which could be seen for miles. There was also a statue of one of the condemned Alice Nutter erected in the nearby village of Roughlee. Coincidentally prior to the anniversary a 17th century cottage was unearthed near the hill which is believed to be Malkin Tower. The skeletal remains of a cat were found within the brick work.

I visited in 2017 and whilst I found the scenic landscape to be beautiful and serene it certainly has a remote, eerie aura about it. To get to the hill itself you just simply follow the Witch Walking Trail from Barley Village which is clearly marked with several little cool witch on broomstick signs. You make your way through several gates, babbling streams, past several farm houses until you're at the foot of the imposing hill. This is where the steep ascent begins. But be warned, I advise you be in pretty good shape as it is a lengthy steep climb and takes real effort to get to the top. Once you've reached the summit at Trig Point however you're rewarded with some fantastic views of the surrounding areas, the villages below and the Black Moss and Ogden Reservoirs either side of the hill.

The descent is equally as strenuous and you have to exercise caution with your footing. If you want a lengthier hike you can make your way across the summit and descend down the other side of the hill which eventually brings you out at the village of Newchurch-In-Pendle but I was pushed for time so just chose to do the climb. You haven't really visited Pendle Hill if you don't make the climb. The village of Newchurch has a cool little shop called Witches Galore which sells a range of books, coffee mugs, chalices and all kinds of witchy paraphernalia. It is also in the village St Mary's church where the supposed tomb of Alice Nutter is located. However this is highly unlikely as there's no way a person executed for witchcraft would be buried on consecrated ground.

A very atmospheric place and well worth a visit.

Statue of one of the convicted witches Alice Nutter.

The sign says it all!

The author at Trig Point Pendle Hill Summit.

Saddleworth Moor

Located in the South Pennines in the Greater Manchester area Saddleworth Moor certainly merits its dark, tragic past. It is a vast, bleak, creepy place with a constant presence of a howling wind. There are four reservoirs on the moor – Dovestone, Yeoman Hey, Greenfield and Chew. The A635 road divides the moor.

In August 1949 a BEA Douglas DC3 aircraft crashed into the moor killing twenty four passengers and crew leaving eight survivors. But what gave Saddleworth Moor its defining notoriety is the infamous 'Moors Murders' committed between July 1963 and October 1965 by partners in crime Ian Brady and Myra Hindley. The bodies of twelve year old John Kilbride, twelve year old Lesley Ann Downey and sixteen year old Pauline Reade were found in various locations on the moor. The body of twelve year old Keith Bennett has never been found. Brady is reluctant to reveal its location.

The murderous pair were both given life sentences. A tape recording of Lesley Ann Downey being tortured was played in court to a shocked audience. Hindley died in prison in 2002 aged sixty of Bronchial Pneumonia. Brady was declared criminally insane in 1985 and died of heart failure in Ashworth Maximum Security Psychiatric Hospital Merseyside on May 15, 2017. He made repeated requests to be transferred to a normal prison where he could end his life by hunger strike and was force fed through a nasal tube.

In a strange twist of events an unidentified body of a man was discovered on the moor in December 2015. The cause of death was revealed to be strychnine poisoning. He was later identified as David Lytton who had flown from Pakistan where he was residing two days prior to his death. It seems he made his way up from London to Saddleworth Moor to take his own life. This in itself remains a mystery as to why someone would go to so much trouble to do this.

Upon visiting the place I can certainly verify that it does indeed have a creepy atmosphere to it. The howling wind is ever present, however the present day busy traffic of the A635 makes it somewhat less isolated. I'm sure it would have been much more desolate in the mid-60's when the infamous crimes were committed.

The Metro commuter newspaper announcing Brady's death.

Established in 1830 and located 60km south east of the Tasmanian capital of Hobart Port Arthur is a convict settlement on the Tasman Peninsula. From 1833 to 1853 it was a destination for the hardest of British criminals. Mainly made up of rebellious personalities from other convict stations and those who reoffended upon arrival in Australia. Inmates were housed in 2 meter square cells in the penitentiary block and subject to brutal hard labour. Disobedient and troublesome inmates were subjected to harsh punishments including lashings and food deprivation. However, the authorities came to the conclusion that punishments such as whippings only served to harden certain inmates therefore psychological torture was introduced.

Convicts would be forced to wear a hood and stay silent, the idea being to give them time to reflect on what they had done and why they were here. A separate prison was established within the grounds in 1850 to house the more violent inmates. This was a building comprising of four wings made up of solitary confinement cells.

The settlement was deemed escape proof as it was totally surrounded by shark infested water. The only access to the mainland was via the Eagleneck Isthmus which was heavily guarded with soldiers and half starved dogs. This was no deterrent to some convicts however and many attempted the escape and were killed in the process. Only three escapees made it to freedom. One of the most notable escape attempts was that of George 'Billy' Hunt who using kangaroo hide disguised himself and attempted to hop across the Isthmus! The guards – living on meagre rations themselves saw this as a potential feast attempted to shoot what they thought was a kangaroo! Hunt, upon seeing them fixing their sights on him promptly threw of the disguise and surrendered. He received 150 lashes for his creative ingenuity.

Juvenile convicts were also sent here. Up to 3,000 boys, many as young as nine were housed at the separate Point Puer Prison during the years the settlement was active. They too were subjected to hard labour. Weekly attendance at the Sunday church service at the prison chapel was compulsory for the entire prison population. The settlement also had its own cemetery in the form of an island known as the 'Isle Of The Dead'. Inmates were seen as nothing and therefore buried in unmarked graves. Only soldiers and prison staff had the privilege of being buried in a marked grave. The prison closed in 1877. It remains Tasmania's biggest tourist attraction.

On April 28, 1996 at approximately 1.30 pm Port Arthur again gained notoriety, this time for a completely different reason. A lone gunman went on the rampage killing 35 people including children and injuring 23. It was the deadliest mass shooting in Australian history. Most murders were committed in the Broad Arrow Café. A total of 20 people were shot at almost point blank range as the café was dealing with a busy Sunday lunch. Others were shot in the surrounding areas as the gunman fled. The perpetrator, intellectually disabled Martin Bryant, was apprehended the next day and is currently serving life without the possibility of parole. The massacre initiated a severe crackdown on the availability of firearms in Australia.

Of course when you have a crime of such magnitude and media attention you're always going to have questions that remain unanswered resulting in the inevitable conspiracy theories. Now, I've looked into this myself and I have to say that there are a lot of things that weren't addressed which should have been. But I'm not going to get into that here. At the end of the day 35 innocent people lost their lives whichever way you slice and dice it.

There are daily trips to Port Arthur from Hobart. The journey takes around ninety minutes which stops at the fantastic sea cliff location of Devil's Kitchen on the way. This is an amazing spot and an ideal location for some great photographs. When you arrive at the Port Arthur Visitor Centre you are given a card which is allocated to an inmate whereupon you can trace his history. The cost of the visit includes a tour of the harbour with an additional cost to explore the Isle Of The Dead if you so wish. Upon arrival you are met by a guide who gives you a short tour of the iconic penitentiary block and brief history of the settlement. You are then free to explore the site at your leisure. There are over thirty buildings and ruins to see on 40 hectares of landscaped ground so allow yourself a minimum of four hours for a thorough exploration. The massacre is still a touchy subject so it's a good idea to refrain from bringing it up with staff as they don't want this tragedy to define this historic site.

The foundation and walls of the Broad Arrow Café remain with a memorial garden and pond out the back. There is also a shrine and a plaque adorned with all the victim's names where you can pay your respects. I did it and believe me the atmosphere hits you like a brick in the face. You can just feel the death within those walls.

Of course with its history Port Arthur is regarded as one of the most haunted places in Australia. So, if you fancy a paranormal experience there are nightly ghost tours around the entire site. An absolute must i

The remains of the Broad Arrow Café.

PORT ARTHUR
MEMORIAL GARDEN

DEDICATED BY

HIS EXCELLENCY THE
HONOURABLE

SIR WILLIAM DEANE, AC, KBE

GOVERNOR-GENERAL OF THE
COMMONWEALTH OF AUSTRALIA,

28TH OF APRIL 2000

WINIFRED APLIN
WALTER BENNETT
NICOLE BURGESS
SOU LENG CHUNG
ELVA GAYLARD
ZOE HALL
ELIZABETH HOWARD
MARY HOWARD
MERVYN HOWARD
RONALD JARY
TONY KISTAN
DENNIS LEVER
SARAH LOUGHTON
DAVID MARTIN
NOELENE (SALLY) MARTIN
PAULINE MASTERS

NANETTE MIKAC
MADELINE MIKAC
ALANNAH MIKAC
ANDREW MILLS
PETER NASH
GWENDA NEANDER
WILLIAM XEENG NG
ANTHONY NIGHTINGALE
MARY NIXON
GLENN PEARS
RUSSELL POLLARD
JANETTE QUIN
HELENE SALZMAN
ROBERT SALZMAN
KATE SCOTT
KEVIN SHARP
ROYCE THOMPSON
JASON WINTER

Memorial plaque for the victims.

Looking at this beautiful picturesque North Yorkshire coastal town it's probably hard to imagine why I would include it in this book. Divided by the River Esk running through the centre of town separating the east and west cliffs overlooking the North Sea, it's one of Britain's most scenic sea towns. Captain James Cook made his voyage from here upon his discovery of Australia and New Zealand. There is a statue in his honour on the west cliffs as well as a museum at his house.

The thought of staying in one of the town's many guest houses on the west cliffs overlooking the ruins of Whitby Abbey perched on top of the east cliffs directly opposite listening to the howling wind and the sea crashing against the ancient walls is simply euphoric. Especially whilst penning ideas for a story in candlelight with a fine bottle of whisky or red wine for company. This is exactly how Bram Stoker got his inspiration whilst writing his ground breaking horror masterpiece Dracula in this very town. Stoker was inspired by the atmospheric setting of the town whilst holidaying in a house on the west cliff in 1890. With the red roofed houses, Whitby Abbey ruins perched on top of the cliff overlooking the roaring sea it really was food for thought. So much so, that he included the town in his story. Dracula's Russian ship is wrecked off the North Yorkshire coast on it's way to London. The only survivor, he emerges from the ship as a big black dog and wreaks havoc on the town.

I've visited Whitby on several occasions and never get tired of the place. In fact, if I had the means and resources I would happily settle there. Walking around the town it's easy to see why Stoker was so inspired as to include it in his masterpiece. It really is the perfect setting for such a story. One has to climb 199 steps to get to St Mary's Church graveyard. But once there you are treated to a spectacular view of the North Sea. Most of the old tombstones are so weathered and blackened by the North Sea winds that the epitaph has been completely erased. They really are a sight to behold. I enjoyed a walk along the west pier which goes all the way to the mouth of the River Esk meeting the North Sea. There are two lighthouse beacons on each of the east and west piers. The west being the taller of the two at 84 feet. It was open to the public on my last visit, and is a steep 81 step climb but once at the top the view overlooking the town, cliffs and sea was simply breathe taking.

I find the town to have a very Lovecraftian atmosphere about it. Witnessing the roaring tide crashing against the ancient sea walls one could imagine it being the perfect setting for a H.P. Lovecraft story such as *The Shadow Over Innsmouth.* Of course Whitby also hosts some fine pubs and cafes. Some say it has the best fish 'n' chips in Britain. Some of the more popular ones include The Magpie Café on Pier Road and Fortunes who have been in the business of smoked kippers for over 135 years. They also specialise in smoked salmon, haddock, bacon and kipper pate. These folks are truly the masters at what they do and once you've tasted their product there's no going back. Souvenir shops selling gifts and crafts are scattered all throughout the alleys and backstreets. Many Dracula novelties can be found here.

Perhaps the main attraction however is the Dracula Experience itself on Marine Parade. A walk in haunted house type tour that depicts the Dracula story using creepy sounds, lighting, special effects and live actors. Maybe a tad on the tacky side but still a lot of fun. Oh and let's not forget the Bram Stoker tribute bench located on the west cliffs with the awesome view that provided the inspiration for his story!

Undoubtedly though what's really put Whitby on the cultural map is the Whitby Goth Weekend music festival held twice yearly in April and late October to coincide with Halloween. WGW started in 1994 and is now one of the biggest alternative festivals in the world. It attracts goths and people of alternative cultures from across the globe. From far and wide the black clad masses descend on this coastal town for four days of sinister partying. The event hosts a whole range of market stalls selling clothing and accessories as well as arts and crafts. There are multi-themed events and even a charity football match held on Sunday afternoon between two Goth teams – now that I've gotta see! Some of the genres most well known acts have played WGW, including The Damned, Rosetta Stone, Switchblade Symphony, Andi Sexgang, Toyah, Alien Sex Fiend and U.K. Decay. The event also brings in huge revenue for the town. Raking in over 1 million pounds per annum.

The town is also host to the Bram Stoker International Film Festival. Now in its eighth year at time of writing the festival is dedicated to continuing Whitby's and Bram Stoker's gothic tradition. It started out as a means to celebrate Bram Stoker's undeniable influence on horror film and literature and is now an annual showcase featuring an array of horror films, lectures, live bands and performance art.

...view that served as an inspiration for Bram Stoker's story Dracula.

THE VIEW FROM THIS SPOT INSPIRED
BRAM STOKER (1847 - 1912)
TO USE WHITBY AS THE SETTING OF PART OF HIS
WORLD - FAMOUS NOVEL
DRACULA
This seat was erected by Scarborough Borough Council
And the Dracula Society to mark the 68th Anniversary
Of Stoker's death - April 20th 1980

Bram Stoker's bench.

Port of Whitby.

Windswept tombstones Whitby Abbey.

Whitby Goth Weekend.

About The Author

Marquis H.K. is a self taught independent writer and accomplished traveller. *Eerie Planet – A Pictorial Study Of Some Of The Darkest Places In History* is his second book. His first being *Thirty Years Of Anger – One Man's Journey Through The Australian Underground Hardcore Punk and Extreme Metal Scenes*. His other previous works include *The Sentinel magazine* and *Slices Of Sin Erotic Comic Book*. He has also been interviewed in various forms of the Australian media including Network Ten's *The Project* discussing Satanism and the Black Arts. His other passions include music and horror movies as well as being an avid collector.

Printed in Great Britain
by Amazon

41381182R00097